Jeff Patterson

This book is presented to you by your Church on the event of your graduation from College. Please accept it as our expression of interest in your life, our joy at your achievement and our conviction that Jesus will prove to be The Most Significant Person in Your Life.

OSCEOLA CHURCH OF THE BRETHREN
Jeffrey Copp, Pastor   6/2/85

Original edition published in English under the title PRAYERS OF JESUS by Lion Publishing, Tring, England, copyright © 1980 Lion Publishing.

First published in the United States and Canada in 1984 by Thomas Nelson Publishers.

Published in Nashville, Tennessee, by Thomas Nelson, Inc. and distributed in Canada by Lawson Falle, Ltd., Cambridge, Ontario.

Photographs by Fritz Fankhauser: pages 12, 14, 26, 35, 36; Fisons Fertilizer Division: page 24 and endpapers; Sonia Halliday Photographs: F. H. C. Birch, page 39 and cover, Sonia Halliday, pages 9, 16, 23, 28, 30, 41, Jane Taylor, 7, 32, 44; Alan Hutchison Library: page 19, Robin Constable, page 21; Lion Publishing: David Alexander, page 10, Jon Willcocks, page 42.

Scripture quotations are from the *Good News Bible*—Old Testament: Copyright © American Bible Society 1976; New Testament: Copyright © American Bible Society 1966, 1971, 1976.

Printed in Shenzhen, China

ISBN 0-8407-5400-0

PRAYERS
OF
JESUS

Thomas Nelson Publishers
Nashville • Camden • New York

MAN OF PRAYER

Crowds of people came to hear him and be healed
from their diseases. But he would go away to
lonely places, where he prayed.

LUKE 5:15-16

The hills of Galilee, where Jesus often prayed.

OUR FATHER

Seeing Jesus pray, his disciples asked him to teach them how to pray. He gave them the pattern prayer which Christians have used down the centuries.

Our Father in heaven:
May your holy name be honored.

GOD'S WILL ON EARTH

May your Kingdom come; may your will be done on earth as it is in heaven.

The village of Maloula in Syria.

ALL WE NEED

Give us today the food we need.

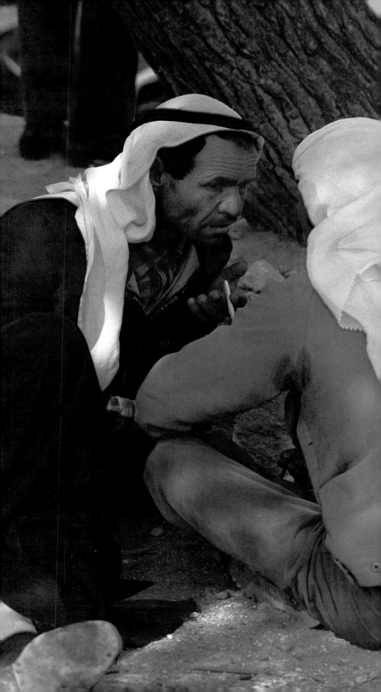

FORGIVENESS

Forgive us the wrongs we have done,
as we forgive the wrongs that others
have done to us. Do not bring us to
hard testing, but keep us safe from
the Evil One.

MATTHEW 6:9-13

JESUS GIVES THANKS

When he was faced with five thousand hungry people,
and only five loaves and two fish to feed them with,
Jesus remained unperturbed. Calmly, as his custom was,
he gave God thanks for the food provided.

Jesus fed the crowds on a hillside in Galilee.

Then Jesus took the five loaves and the two fish, looked up to heaven, and gave thanks to God. He broke the loaves and gave them to his disciples to distribute to the people. He also divided the two fish among them all. Everyone ate and had enough.

MARK 6:41-42

JESUS REJOICES

Jesus sent out seventy-two of his followers. They were to
go ahead of him, two by two, to every town and place
where he was about to go. They were to heal the sick
and tell people of God's kingdom: that Jesus had come to
begin a new age. The seventy-two returned with joy,
telling how even the demons submitted to them in
Christ's name. Jesus shared their joy, praising God:

Father, Lord of heaven and earth! I thank you
because you have shown to the unlearned what you
have hidden from the wise and learned. Yes, Father,
this was how you were pleased to have it happen.

LUKE 10:21

JESUS BLESSES THE CHILDREN

People brought their children to Jesus, wanting him to ask God's blessing on them. When the disciples tried to protect him from their demands, turning people away, Jesus was angry.

"Let the children come to me, and do not stop them, because the Kingdom of God belongs to such as these. I assure you that whoever does not receive the Kingdom of God like a child will never enter it." Then he took the children in his arms, placed his hands on each of them, and blessed them.

MARK 10:14-16

LAZARUS LIVES

Jesus' friend Lazarus had died. His sisters could not understand why Jesus had not arrived in time to heal him. They had not yet learned that his power extends beyond the grave. Jesus ordered the people to take away the stone that sealed the entrance to the tomb. Then he prayed to God.

"I thank you, Father, that you listen to me. I know that you always listen to me, but I say this for the sake of the people here, so that they will believe that you sent me." After he had said this, he called out in a loud voice, "Lazarus, come out!" He came out, his hands and feet wrapped in grave cloths, and with a cloth around his face. "Untie him," Jesus told them, "and let him go."

JOHN 11:41-44

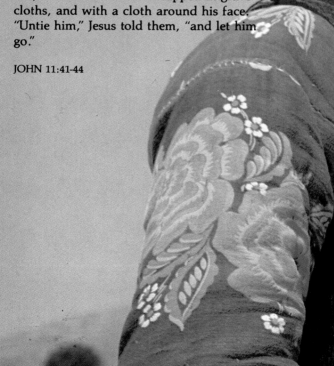

FACING DEATH

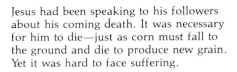

Jesus had been speaking to his followers about his coming death. It was necessary for him to die—just as corn must fall to the ground and die to produce new grain. Yet it was hard to face suffering.

Now my heart is troubled—and what shall I say? Shall I say, "Father, do not let this hour come upon me?" But that is why I came—so that I might go through this hour of suffering. Father, bring glory to your name!

JOHN 12:27-28

ETERNAL LIFE

On the eve of his death, in the upper room with the little group of his close friends, Jesus prayed—for himself, for his friends, and for all who would believe in him.

Father, the hour has come. Give glory to your Son, so that the Son may give glory to you. For you gave him authority over all mankind, so that he might give eternal life to all those you gave him. And eternal life means to know you, the only true God, and to know Jesus Christ, whom you sent.

JOHN 17:1-3

Houses built in a traditional style, in a village in Israel.

THE FINISHED WORK

I have shown your glory on earth; I
have finished the work you gave me
to do. Father! Give me glory in your
presence now, the same glory I had
with you before the world was made.

JOHN 17:4-5

ALL ONE

I pray for them. I do not pray for the world but for
those you gave me, for they belong to you. All I
have is yours, and all you have is mine; and my
glory is shown through them. And now I am

Women gathering olives in Tunisia.

coming to you; I am no longer in the world, but they are in the world. Holy Father! Keep them safe by the power of your name, the name you gave me, so that they may be one just as you and I are one.

JOHN 17:9-11

KEPT SAFE

I do not ask you to take them out of the world, but
I do ask you to keep them safe from the Evil One.
Just as I do not belong to the world, they do not
belong to the world. Dedicate them to yourself by
means of the truth; your word is truth. I sent them
into the world, just as you sent me into the world.

JOHN 17:15-18

A crowded street in the old city of Jerusalem.

GETHSEMANE

On the night of his betrayal, Jesus took
his friends to a quiet orchard of
olive-trees. In great agony of mind, he
prayed—about the cup of suffering he was
about to drink, the death he was about to
die. For he was to take onto his own
shoulders the burden of the world's sin.

My Father, if it is possible, take this
cup of suffering from me! Yet not
what I want, but what you want.

MATTHEW 26:39

An ancient olive tree in the Garden of
Gethsemane.

FORGIVE THEM

Outside the city of Jerusalem, at the place called The Skull, Jesus was crucified between two criminals. At the point of his death, he prayed for his enemies.

Forgive them, Father! They don't know what they are doing.

LUKE 23:34

The Golden Gate and city walls, Jerusalem.

ALONE

On the cross, Jesus took on himself the weight of human sin, the horror of separation from God the Father. He cried out in an agony of pain and loneliness.

My God, my God, why did you abandon me?

MATTHEW 27:46

LAST WORDS

Jesus' dying breath, as he hung on the
cross, was a prayer to God.

Father! In your hands, I place my
spirit!

LUKE 23:46

THE RISEN CHRIST

Two days later, on the first Easter Sunday, two of Jesus'
disciples were walking along a road talking of Jesus'
death and the rumor that he was alive again. A stranger
joined them, and as they reached the village was invited
to stay. It was as he thanked God for the evening meal
that they realized he was Jesus.

He sat down to eat with them, took the bread, and said the blessing; then he broke the bread and gave it to them. Then their eyes were opened and they recognized him.

LUKE 24:30-31

THE ASCENSION

Jesus appeared to his disciples over a period of forty days after his resurrection. When the time came for him to return to his Father, his last action was to pray God's blessing on them all.

Then he led them out of the city as far as Bethany, where he raised his hands and blessed them. As he was blessing them, he departed from them and was taken up into heaven.

LUKE 24:50-51

The village of Bethany, close to Jerusalem.